Contents

5 - Introduction

5 - Author's Note

6 - Salad Dressing
7 - Parsley Sauce
8 - Fairy Toast
9 - Mayonnaise
10 - Dried Hard Boiled Egg
11 - Stuffing
12 - Leek Pudding
13 - Economy Sausage Rolls
14 - Cheese Frizzles
15 - Mock Cocktail Sausages
17 - Celery Pie
18 - Carrot Curry
19 - Vegetable Soup
20 - Bread Omlette
21 - Woolton Pie
23 - Cauliflower Leaves and Breadcrumbs
24 - Cabbage with Horseradish
27 - Mock Oysters
28 - Fish Pastry
29 - Mock Fish
30 - Mock Lobster
31 - Toad in the Hole
33 - Beef a'la Mode
34 - Mock Turkey
35 - Mock Pork Chops
36 - Spam Fritters
38 - Mock Duck
39 - Liver and Bacon
40 - Corned Beef Pudding

42 - Spam Pie
43 - Mock Goose
46 - Pea Bread
47 - Scones
48 - Carrot Fudge
49 - Scotch Dumpling
50 - Wartime Custard
52 - Chocolate Pudding
53 - Potato Pudding
54 - Mock Bananas
55 - Trifle
56 - Carrot Pastries
57 - Whip
58 - Sponge
59 - Potato Fudge
61 - National Loaf
62 - Economy Bread
63 - Currant Biscuits
64 - Spice Biscuits
65 - Fruit Pie
66 - Carrot Biscuits
67 - Cream
68 - Icing
69 - Economy Cake
70 - Christmas Cake
71 - Marzipan
72 - Beetroot Dessert
73 - Carrolade
74 - Fruit Tea
75 - Apple Water

Ration Book Christmas Cookbook

Margaret Harper

© Copyright 2021 Margaret Harper.
All rights Reserved.

Introduction

World War 2 saw rationing of food and other items in Britain. The war effort plus a blockade of imported food to Britain led to shortages.

Many foods such as bananas were not available. Other basic foods - such as meat, sugar and eggs - were rationed. The rationing system insured everyone had enough to eat and a nutritious diet, but it led to a more blander diet with many familiar items not being available. Christmas, a time when more food than usual is consumed, suffered with traditional Christmas items such as turkey, chocolate and many alcoholic drinks unavailable. Instead people had to make to with alternative Christmas foods substituting foods such as vegetable or oatmeal for meat products.

Try some rationing Christmas dishes with this book - Ration Book Christmas Cookbook

Author's Note

This book contains a series of recipes that were eaten in Britain between 1939-45 at Christmas time. I wrote the book because I am interested in the period of rationing between 1939-45 and the types of food eaten. There are a lot of historical records on the food eaten in the period and I hope I have managed to recreate some of the dishes eaten. I have ensured that all ingredients and cooking utensils needed are able to be bought in contemporary stores.

Salad Dressing

Ingredients

300ml/1 and quarter cups of milk
85g/3 oz of grated raw beetroot
1 tablespoon of vinegar
85g/3 oz of flour
sugar
salt
pepper

Mix the flour and milk and make a sauce. Add some sugar, beetroot and some salt and pepper and mix.

Parsley Sauce

Ingredients

300ml/1 and a quarter cups of milk
1 tablespoon of margarine
1 tablespoon of cornflour/cornstarch
3 teaspoons of chopped fresh parsley
salt
pepper

Put the margarine in a pan and melt. Add the cornflour and mix to make a paste. Add the milk and stir, then cook for 4 minutes stirring all the time. Add the parsley and some salt and pepper.

Fairy Toast

Ingredients

thin slices of stale wholemeal bread

Put the bread on a baking sheet. Cook in preheated oven at 190C/375F for 20 minutes- until browned.

Mayonnaise

Ingredients

1 teaspoon of wet mustard
1 teaspoon of vinegar
1 cooked and mashed potato
100ml/3.3 fl oz of oil
salt
pepper

Mix the ingredients with some salt and pepper to make a smooth mix.

Dried Hard Boiled Egg

Ingredients

dried egg
water

Make up the dried egg using 1 tablespoon of egg to 2 tablespoons of water for one egg.

Put the egg into greased ramekins/moulds. Put the moulds in a pan of hot water - with enough water to come up to half the level of the moulds. Then cook on a low heat for 13 minutes.

Leave the egg to cool. Serve in same way as hard boiled eggs.

Stuffing

Ingredients

2 chopped onions
141g/5 oz of dried breadcrumbs
141g/5 oz of chopped celery
2 tablespoons of melted margarine or lard
salt
pepper

Mix the ingredients. Use some hot water to mix if too dry.

Stuff a bird with the mix or cook in a greased baking dish in a preheated oven at 190C/375F for 20 minutes.

Leek Pudding

Ingredients

2 chopped leeks
255g/9 oz of flour
85g/3 oz of suet
85g/3 oz of raw grated potato
1 teaspoon of sodium bicarbonate/baking soda
salt
pepper

Put the flour, suet and potato in a bowl. Add some water to make a dough.

Roll out the dough. Line a pudding bowl with some dough. Layer the leek in the bowl adding salt and pepper. Top with dough.

Cover the bowl with parchment paper and tie with string.

Put a bowl or upside down colander in a saucepan. Fill with water to just cover the bowl. Put the pudding bowl on top, cover then cook on a low heat for 2 hours.

Economy Sausage Rolls

Ingredients

4 carrots
mashed potato
3 tablespoons of oatmeal
vegetable extract

Chop the carrots and place in a pan of boiling water. Cook on a low heat for 9 minutes. Add the oatmeal and vegetable extract. Cook for 6 minutes. Drain the carrot mix and chop with a knife.

Roll out the mashed potato. Cut into rectangle shapes. Put some of the carrot mix on top of the shapes and roll them up.

Cook in a preheated oven at 200C/392F for 35 minutes.

Cheese Frizzles

Ingredients

3 tablespoons of grated cheese
3 tablespoons of oatmeal
a quarter of a teaspoon of baking soda/sodium bicarbonate
pepper
salt
oil

Mix the cheese, oatmeal and baking soda in a bowl with some salt and pepper. Add some water and make a stiff mix.

Put spoonfuls of the mix into a pan of hot oil and cook until browned on both sides.

Mock Cocktail Sausages

Ingredients

2 chopped potatoes
1 chopped cabbage
50g/1 cup of wholemeal breadcrumbs

Put the potatoes in boiling water, then cook on a low heat for 12 minutes - until cooked. Drain.

Put the cabbage in a pan of hot water. Cover and cook on a low heat for 15 minutes. Drain.

Mix all the ingredients. Shape into cocktail sausages then fry in oil until cooked.

Wartime Christmas Food Facts

American soldiers stationed in Britain often stayed with British families for Christmas. These soldiers were various food supplies by the US government which they were able to share with their British hosts. Foods included items such as fruit juice, evaporated milk, bacon, sugar, coffee, lard, rice and peas.

American soldiers based in Britain during the war would often hold a Christmas party at their base for local children with a range of food they had brought over.

Christmas during WW2 was a different time for many families. Children were often living away from home having been evacuated from the cities. And of course members of the family were away fighting in the war. Many had to spend much of Christmas in an air raid shelter. But people tried to make the best of it with gatherings, parties and listening to special Christmas programmes on the radio.

During World War 2 food such as butter, meat etc could be bought on the black market at a higher price than usual. Some shopkeepers kept black market food for special customers and "spivs" traded in black market food and other items. But this was illegal and people caught doing it were prosecuted.

Celery Pie

Ingredients

6 sticks of chopped celery
130ml/4.4 fl oz of dried milk made up
1 tablespoon of dried egg mixed with 2 tablespoons of water
3 tablespoons of grated cheese
pastry
salt

Put the celery in a pan. Cover with lightly salted water and cook on a low heat for 8 minutes.

Line a dish with pastry. Place in a medium oven for 10 minutes.

Mix the egg and milk. Put the celery in the pastry dish. Add the egg and milk mix. Cook in a medium oven for 15 minutes- until the egg is set.

Carrot Curry

Ingredients

700g/1 and a half lb of chopped carrots
half a chopped onion
300ml/10 fl oz of water
1 teaspoon of allspice
half a tablespoon of jam
2 teaspoons of curry powder
1 teaspoon of vegetable extract
salt
pepper
margarine

Put the carrots in a pan of boiling water, then cook on a low heat for 8 minutes. Drain the carrots. The water can be reserved for adding to the curry.

Fry the onion in some margarine for 8 minutes. Add the curry powder, allspice, jam and vegetable extract. Mix, then cook for 5 minutes. Add the water (or carrot water) and some salt and pepper. Cook on a low heat for 15 minutes. Add the carrots and cook on a low heat for another 12 minutes.

Vegetable Soup

Ingredients

400g/14 oz of chopped cabbage
1 chopped carrot
1 tablespoon of dried milk
2 tablespoons of flour
1 teaspoon of salt
1 litre/4 cups of vegetable stock

Boil the stock then add the cabbage, carrot and salt. Cook on a low heat for 15 minutes.

Add the flour and dried milk. Mix, then cook on a low hear for 6 minutes.

Bread Omlette

Ingredients

4 slices of wholemeal bread
2 tablespoons of dried egg mixed with 4 tablespoons of water
dried milk
margarine

Put the dried milk in a bowl with some water. Add the bread and leave for 7 minutes.

Drain the bread. Put the bread in a pan with some margarine and cook for 4 minutes - breaking the bread up. Add the egg and cook for 7 minutes - until the egg is set.

Woolton Pie

Ingredients

400g/14 oz of chopped carrot
400g/14 oz of chopped potato
400g/14 oz of chopped Swede/Rutabaga
400g/14 oz of chopped cauliflower
1 tablespoon of oatmeal
1 teaspoon of vegetable extract
pastry
parsley

Put the vegetable extract, carrot, swede, cauliflower and potato in a saucepan and cover with water. Cook on a low heat for 12 minutes.

Put the mix in a pie dish lined with pastry. Put some parsley on top and cover with pastry. Cook on a preheated oven at 176C/350F for 15 minutes.

Wartime Christmas Food Facts

In 1942 soap was added to the list of rationed items. People often saved some of their soap ration so they could have extra at Christmas or give it as a gift.

Every person was given a ration book with coupons to purchase goods. Foods such as sugar, bacon, cheese, meat and lard were rationed via a coupon book.

Other items such as dried fruit biscuits, cereals and tinned goods were rationed via a points system - with the number of points given according to the current supply of the food.

Bread was not rationed during the war. It was rationed after World War 2 ended.

A special bread loaf was introduced called the National Loaf. This was a brown loaf made from wholemeal flour and created because of shortages of white flour and to allow more wheat to be used elsewhere. Many people were not fans of the loaf!

In January 1940 bacon and ham, butter, jam and sugar were rationed. Fresh meat rationed from March 1940. Cheese was rationed from spring 1941. From July 1942 sweets were rationed. People were allowed 12 oz per month.

Cauliflower Leaves and Breadcrumbs

Ingredients

cauliflower leaves
breadcrumbs
oil
salt

Put the leaves in some boiling salted water and cook on a low heat for 10 minutes - until tender.

Drain the cauliflower and coat in breadcrumbs. Fry in hot oil for 6 minutes,

Cabbage with Horseradish

Ingredients

900g/2 lbs of chopped cooked cabbage
28g/1 oz of margarine
28g/1 oz of flour
250ml/1 cup of milk
250ml/1 cup of vegetable stock or water cabbage was cooked in.
3 tablespoons of grated horseradish
1 tablespoon of vinegar

Mix the margarine and stock in a pan and cook for 4 minutes. Add the milk and stir. Cook on a low heat for 6 minutes.

Add the horseradish and vinegar.

Put the cabbage in a bowl and pour over the horseradish.

Woolton Pie

Economy Sausage Rolls

Toad in the Hole

Spam Fritters

Mock Oysters

Ingredients

5 sardines with bones taken out and skin taken off
5 cooked artichokes
4 tablespoons of milk
salt
pepper
dried breadcrumbs

Take the artichokes and run them through a sieve.

Mix the artichoke with the rest of the ingredients. Put the mix in ramekins or empty scallop shells. Sprinkle over breadcrumbs.

Place in a preheated oven at 190C/375F for 10 minutes - until browned on top.

Fish Pastry

Ingredients

255g/9 oz of cooked fish
255g/9 oz of chopped cooked vegetables
500ml/2 cups of white sauce
1 tablespoon of vinegar
salt
pepper
pastry
parsley

Mix the vegetables, fish, parsley, white sauce, vinegar and some salt and pepper in a bowl.

Roll out the pastry. Cut into circles. Put some of the fish mix in the middle of each circle. Fold over the pastry encasing the fish mix.

Cook in a preheated oven at 190C/375F for 30 minutes.

Mock Fish

Ingredients

85g/3 oz of ground rice
260ml/1 cup of milk
1 tablespoon of finely chopped onion
1 tablespoon of dried egg mixed with 2 tablespoons of water
1 tablespoon of margarine
wholemeal breadcrumbs
drop of anchovy essence
extra milk and margarine or oil

Put the milk in a pan and bring to the boil. Add the rice, margarine, onion and anchovy. Cook on a low heat for 18 minutes.

Take off the heat and add the egg. Mix well. Spread the mix on a plate and leave to cool.

Cut into fish fillet sized pieces. Coat with some milk and coat in breadcrumbs. Fry in margarine or oil on both sides until browned.

Mock Lobster

Ingredients

255g/9 oz of flaked white fish with no bones or skin
4 tablespoons of creamy salad dressing
1 tablespoon of tomato ketchup/sauce
1 teaspoon of Worcester sauce
1 teaspoon of sugar
salt
pepper
parsley

Mix the ingredients.

Toad in the Hole

Ingredients

400g/14 oz of chopped meat - e.g. sausages
113g/4 oz of flour
1 tablespoon of dried egg mixed with 2 tablespoons of water
360ml/1 and a half cups of water mixed with 4 tablespoons of dried milk powder
salt
margarine

Cook the meat in a frying pan for 10 minutes.

Mix the flour, egg and water to make a batter. Add some salt.

Preheat an oven to 200C/400F. Put some margarine in a baking dish and melt the margarine in the oven. Add the meat to the dish and pour over the batter. Cook in the oven for 30 minutes.

Wartime Christmas Food Facts

Vegetables played a big part in the wartime diet and people were encouraged to grow at home and in places such as parks as part of a community effort as part of a "dig for Victory" campaign. As a result vegetables played a big part in the Christmas menu.

Preserving fruit and jam making was done on a large scale during World War 2 in order to make the most of any fruit grown, and of course take advantage of wild food such as blackberries.

Every year the British Ministry of Food released a selection of Christmas recipe suggestions from available ingredients. Radio programmes, leaflets and magazine and newspaper articles gave tips on Christmas cooking on rationing.

During wartime basic goods such as toys, clothing, cotton and metal became scarce. So gifts made from these items could not often be given. Instead more simple gifts were given or practical gifts.

Wrapping paper was not available so gifts were wrapped in newspapers cloth or brown paper. War bonds were a popular gift. Other gifts included homemade chutney and jam, jumpers, hats and scarves using old wool, homemade garden tools, garden fertilizer, garden seeds and even soap.

Coffee was not rationed as Britons did not drink a lot of coffee at the time so there was always enough available.

Beef a'la Mode

Ingredients

450g/15 oz of chopped beef
2 sliced onions
2 sliced carrots
40g/1.4 oz of margarine
1 tablespoon of vinegar
salt
pepper

Put the beef in a bowl. Add a layer of onion and carrot. Add the vinegar. Cover and leave for 10 hours.

Put the margarine in a saucepan. Add the beef and cook for 6 minutes. Add the onion and carrots. Add enough water to cover the mix and some salt and pepper. Cook on a low heat for 5 hours.

Mock Turkey

Ingredients

700g/1 and a half lb of sausage meat
10 thin bacon slices
1 grated apple
1 grated onion
1 grated parsnip
12 slices of stale wholemeal bread turned into breadcrumbs
1 egg
salt
pepper
thyme
parsley

Mix the sausage meat, bread, onion, apple, egg, some salt and pepper and some chopped parsley and thyme in a bowl.

Put the mix on a greased baking tray and shape like a turkey. Put bacon slices on top. Cook in a preheated oven at 176C/350F for 1 hour 15 minutes.

Mock Pork Chops

Ingredients

450g/1 lb of chopped potatoes
170g/6 oz of chopped carrots
4 tablespoons of flour
2 teaspoons of chutney
parsley
oil
salt
pepper

Put the carrots and potatoes in a pan and cover with water. Bring to the boil then cook on a low heat for 10 minutes - until cooked.

Drain the vegetables and mash.

Put 4 tablespoons of flour, salt and pepper, 2 teaspoons of chutney and some chopped parsley in the bowl with the mash and mix.
Shape into pork chop shapes and fry in oil on both sides until cooked.

Spam Fritters

Ingredients

sliced spam
120g/4.2 oz of flour
130ml/half a cup of milk
salt
oil

Mix the flour and milk to make a batter and add some salt and pepper.

Put the spam sliced in the batter, then fry in hot oil on both sides until cooked.

Wartime Christmas Food Facts

Many saved some items in their rations from earlier in the year to use in Christmas dishes.

Turkey, the popular British Christmas dinner dish, was not available during the war years. Instead for Christmas dinner people had chicken, goose, lamb, pork or rabbit. Later in the war these items were often unavailable so a mock meat dish using vegetables would be eaten instead.

Many foodstuffs became short during the war so dishes would be bulked out with substitutes using items such as vegetables and oats. These were termed "mock" dishes. For example mock fudge was made from carrot.

There was a shortage of alcoholic drinks during World War 2. Beer was produced as it was considered to be a good morale booster. Shortages meant that beer was weaker than usual.

Traditional British Christmas foods of turkey, fruit, chocolate and gin were not easily available during the war so alternatives had to be found found.

Boxing Day - December 26 - had been a public holiday in Britain since 1871. But during the war factory and shop workers had to return to work on the 26 as their work was very important for the war effort.

Mock Duck

Ingredients

850g/1.8 lb of sausage meat (or other cheap chopped meat)
400g/14 oz of peeled and grated sour or cooking apples - e.g. Granny Smith or Bramley
400g/14 oz of grated onion
2 teaspoons of sage

Put half the meat mix in a baking dish. Spread the onion, sage and apple on top. Put the rest of the meat on top. The mix can be shaped like a bird breast.

Cover with parchment paper greased with margarine. Cook in a preheated oven at 190C/375F for 50 minutes.

Liver and Bacon

Ingredients

400g/14 oz of liver
200g/7 oz of cooked rice
200g/7 oz of bacon
130ml/half a cup of stock
120g/4 oz of flour
salt
pepper

Fry the bacon in pan for 10 minutes - until cooked. Remove the bacon. Fry the liver in the pan for 10 minutes. Remove the liver.

Put the flour in the pan and stir. Add the stock stirring all the time. Bring to the boil. Add some salt and pepper.

Put the rice on a dish. Add the liver and bacon. Pour over the sauce.

Corned Beef Pudding

Ingredients

400g/14 oz of chopped corned beef (the British canned variety)
3 tablespoons of grated carrot
85g/3 oz of fine oatmeal
85g/3 oz of wholemeal breadcrumbs
2 teaspoons of dried sage
30g/1 oz of lard
200ml/7 fl oz of water or stock
salt
pepper

Put the lard and oatmeal in a pan and cook for 5 minutes. Add the corned beef, sage, breadcrumbs and some salt and pepper. Add the water/stock and stir.

Put the mix in a greased bowl. Wrap in parchment paper and tie with some string. Put an unturned bowl or colander in a pan. Add enough water to just cover the bowl. Add the pudding bowl on top, cover and cook for 1 and half hours.

Wartime Christmas Food Facts

There were no Christmas lights or many of the usual decorations for the Christmas tree during wartime, so decorations made of newspaper and green items from the garden such as holly were used.

The government advised people to dip holly and other green plants in Epsom salts to give them a frosted appearance.

The government provided an alternative idea for fruit at Christmas: vegetables!

Tea and sugar rations were often increased at Christmas time.

Game and pigeon meats were not rationed, but supplies were limited.

Spam was popular during the war as a cheap meat. Supplies came from the USA.

Powdered egg, imported from the US, was a staple item during the war as there was a shortage or real eggs.

For Christmas 1943 it was estimated by the British government's Ministry of food that only one in ten families had the traditional goose or turkey for dinner and had to have mock dishes - e.g. mutton or vegetable substitutes - instead.

Spam Pie

Ingredients

2 cans of spam
400g/14 oz of whole wheat flour
150g/6 oz of mashed potato
100g/4 oz of margarine
1 tablespoon of oatmeal
1 chopped potato
1 chopped carrot
milk
salt
pepper
half a teaspoon of baking soda/sodium bicarbonate

For the pastry mix the mashed potato, flour, baking soda, margarine and some salt in a bowl. Make a dough, using some water if needed.

Put the carrot, oats, some salt and pepper and potato in a pan of boiling water then cook on a low heat for 10 minutes. Drain.

Mix the vegetable mix with the spam.

Roll out the dough. Line a pie dish with pastry. Add the spam mix. Top with pastry and brush with milk.

Cook in a preheated oven at 200C/392F for 35 minutes.

Mock Goose

Ingredients

400g/14 oz of sausage meat
500g/1.1 lb of peeled boiled potatoes
1 chopped onion
gravy
salt
pepper

Put the onions in a pan and cover with water. Bring to the boil. Drain the onions and keep the water.

Mash the potatoes.

In a baking dish, put a layer of onion, then a layer of sausage meat, followed by a layer of potato. Add some salt and pepper.

Make three holes in the mash and pour gravy over the top. Cook in a preheated oven at 190C/375F for 1 hour

Tinned Corned Beef

Carrot Fudge

Potato Fudge

Christmas Cake

Pea Bread

Ingredients

250g/9 oz of tinned peas
250g/9 oz of tomato soup
120g/1 cup of breadcrumbs
1 egg
240ml/1 cup of milk
salt
pepper

Drain the peas. Mash them a little. Put them in a bowl with the rest of the ingredients and mix well. Put in a greased baking tin. Cook on a low heat for 45 minutes.

Scones

Ingredients

280g/10 oz of flour
550ml/2 and 1 third cups of water
4 tablespoons of dried milk
1 dried egg made from 1 tablespoon of dried egg and 2 tablespoons of water
1 and a half tablespoons of sugar
1 teaspoon of sodium bicarbonate/baking soda
margarine

Mix the dried milk and water.

Mix the flour, sodium bicarbonate and salt. Add the milk, egg and sugar. Make a batter.

Put some margarine in a frying pan. Put spoonfuls of the mix in the pan. Cook for 4 minutes on each side - until browned.

Carrot Fudge

Ingredients

5 tablespoons of grated carrot
1 leaf/half a teaspoon of gelatine
drop of orange essence

Make up the gelatine. Put in a bowl with the carrot and some orange essence. Put in a dish and leave to cool. Once hardened cut into chunks.

Scotch Dumpling

Ingredients

350g/12 oz of chopped dried fruit
230ml/1 cup of water
130g/4.5 oz of sugar
2 tablespoons of allspice
230g/8 oz of margarine
250g/9 oz of flour
1 teaspoon of sodium bicarbonate/baking soda
2 tablespoons of dried egg

Mix the dried egg with 6 tablespoons of water.

Put the sugar, allspice, fruit, water and margarine in a pan. boil, then cook on a low heat for 1 minute.

Remove from the heat then add the sodium bicarbonate, eggs and flour and mix.

Wrap in parchment paper, then a baking cloth. tie with string.

Place in a pan of boiling water. cover and cook on a low heat for 2 and a half hours.

Remove pudding. Take off paper and cloth, then place on a baking tray and cook in a preheated medium oven for 15 minutes.

Wartime Custard

Ingredients

2 tablespoons of dried egg
1 tablespoon of sugar
1 pint of milk
nutmeg

Mix the egg, milk and sugar. Add three tablespoons of milk to the egg mix and make a smooth mix. Put the rest of the milk in a pan and bring to the boil. Pour onto the egg mix, stirring all the time. Put the mix back in the pan and cook on a low heat for 6 minutes. Stir, then add some nutmeg.

Wartime Christmas Food Facts

Potatoes were a staple part of the diet and were not rationed - mainly as they could be grown in Britain.

Fruits which were produced outside of Britain such as bananas disappeared from the shops. This was because it was more difficult to import goods by sea because of the German blockade.

Fish was not rationed, but often there was not enough fish for everyone to buy. A South African fish called snoek was readily available in tins, but it was not very popular.

Salt was not rationed during WW2.

Vegetarians were given extra cheese in place of meat in their rations.

Traditional British Christmas cakes and puddings contain dried fruit. As dried fruit was often not available in large quantities as the war went on items such as grated carrot and stale breadcrumbs were used to replace some of the dried fruit.

It is said that because of a lack of raw materials child's toys were either expensive or of poor quality. So people had to be creative for gifts for children.

Chocolate Pudding

Ingredients

custard (see Wartime Custard recipe)
cocoa powder

Add some cocoa powder to the custard and mix well.

Potato Pudding

Ingredients

200g/7 oz of mashed potato
28g/2 oz of margarine
28g/2 oz of sugar
1 tablespoon of dried egg made up with 2 tablespoons of water/or 1 egg
500ml/2 cups of water
3 tablespoons of dried milk
1 tablespoon of jam

Mix the margarine and potato. Add the egg and sugar. Mix the water and milk powder. Add to the potato mix with the jam and mix well.

Put in a greased pie dish and cook in a preheated oven at 190C/375F for 35 minutes.

Mock Bananas

Ingredients

parsnips
banana essence
sugar
margarine

Peel and cut the parsnips into slices. Put on a baking tray and dot with margarine. Cook in a preheated oven at 200C/392F for 40 minutes.

Mash the parsnips in a bowl with some sugar and banana essence to taste.

Trifle

Ingredients

4 stale sweet buns/sweet rolls
cooked fruit such as apples
fruit juice
custard (see custard in this book)

Chop up the buns and place in a bowl.

Put the custard and fruit juice in a pan and cook on a medium heat for 8 minutes. Pour over the buns. Top with the fruit.

Carrot Pastries

Ingredients

255g/9 oz of flour
85g/3 oz of lard or margarine
3 tablespoons of chopped fresh mint
5 tablespoons of grated carrot
85g/3 oz of sugar

Put the carrot in a pan of boiling water. Cook on a low heat for 8 minutes - until cooked. Drain the carrot.

Mix the flour and lard to make a dough. Roll out the dough and divide into two pieces.

Put one half of the pastry in a tin. Mix the mint, carrot and sugar and put spread this over the pastry. Put the other half of pastry on top.

Make a small hole in the centre of the pastry. Cook in a preheated oven at 190C/375F for 20 minutes.

Cut into squares.

Whip

Ingredients

400g/14 oz of de-stoned plums
3 tablespoons of dried milk
3 tablespoons of marmalade

Put the plums in a pan, cover with water, boil, then cook on a low heat for 10 minutes. Drain.

Mash the plums in a bowl with the milk and marmalade and mix well. Serve with fruit or jam

Sponge

Ingredients

1 grated potato
8 grated carrots
1 tablespoon of flour
2 tablespoons of sugar
1 drop of vanilla essence
2 tablespoons of jam

Heat up a bowl. Run the jam on it. Cool.

Mix the rest of ingredients and add to the bowl. Cover with parchment paper greased with margarine and put some string around the bowl to secure the paper.

Put a bowl upside down in a big saucepan. Add enough water to cover the bowl. Put the bowl with the sponge on top of the bowl in the pan. Cover and cook on a low heat for 2 hours.

Potato Fudge

Ingredients

140g/5 oz of cocoa
1 mashed potato
1 teaspoon of sugar
140g/5 oz of margarine

Mix the ingredients to make a dough. Cut into pieces.

Wartime Christmas Food Facts

An example basic weekly food ration for one adult (rations fluctuated during the war):

Bacon & Ham 4 oz Other meat value of 1 shilling and 2 pence (equivalent to 2 chops)
Butter 2 oz
Cheese 2 oz
Margarine 4 oz
Cooking fat 4 oz
Milk 3 pints
Sugar 8 oz
Preserves 1 lb every 2 months
Tea 2 oz
Eggs 1 fresh egg (plus allowance of dried egg)
Sweets 12 oz every 4 weeks

Christmas trees were hard to find as timber was rationed. Homemade ones were often made.

A woman commented on the availability of Christmas food in December 1943:

'We are pretty well on our beam ends as far as Christmas fare is concerned. No chance of turkey, chicken or goose - not even the despised rabbit. If we can get a little mutton that is the best we can hope for. A few Christmas puddings are about. There are shops with three puddings and 800 registered customers.'

National Loaf

Ingredients

300g/10 oz of potato flour
300g/10 oz of wholemeal flour
130ml/half a cup of water
1 crushed vitamin C tablet
1 tablespoon of dried yeast put in a little warm water for 10 minutes
half a teaspoon of sea salt

Mix the ingredients. Place in a greased bowl and cover with a damp cloth. Leave for 2 hours.

Place in a bread tin. Cook in a preheated oven at 200C/400F for 40 minutes.

Economy Bread

Ingredients

500g/1 lb of wholemeal flour
1 tablespoon of dried yeast
1 tablespoon of treacle
110ml/half a cup of warm water

Mix the ingredients and make a dough.

Knead for 15 minutes.

Coat a bowl with vegetable oil. Place the dough int he bowl, top with a damp dishcloth and leave for 2 and a half hours.

Place in a bread tin - or form into rolls and place on a greased baking sheet. Cook in a preheated oven at 200C/400F for 40 minutes.

Currant Biscuits

Ingredients

56g/2 oz of currants
113g/4 oz of margarine
5 tablespoons of milk
1 tablespoon of sodium bicarbonate/baking soda
255g/9 oz of flour
half a teaspoon of mixed spice powder

Put the milk and sugar in a pan. Cook for 6 minutes - until the sugar dissolves. Add the sodium bicarbonate. Take off the heat and cool.

Put the flour in a bowl and mix with the margarine and some salt. Add the mixed spice and currants. Add the milk mix and make a dough.

Roll out the dough and cut out biscuit/cookie shapes.

Cook in a preheated oven at 200C/392F for 12 minutes.

Spice Biscuits

Ingredients

80g/2.8 oz of margarine
2 tablespoons of sugar
80g/6.3 oz of flour
2 tablespoons of honey
2 teaspoons of cinnamon

Mix the margarine and sugar together to make a paste. Add the honey. Add the cinnamon and flour and make a dough.

Roll out the dough. Cut out biscuit/cookie shapes.

Put on a greased baking tray and cook in a preheated oven at 157C/315F for 10 minutes.

Fruit Pie

Ingredients

800g/1.7 lb of fruit - e.g. apples, blackberries
bread cut into cubes
4 tablespoons of milk
3 tablespoon of sugar

Put the bread in a pie dish. Put the bread on top. Pour the milk on the bread and coat the bread with sugar.

Cook in a preheated oven at 157C/315F for 30 minutes.

Carrot Biscuits

Ingredients

9 tablespoons of grated carrot
2 tablespoons of margarine
4 tablespoons of sugar
13 tablespoons of flour
1 teaspoon of sodium bicarbonate/baking soda
half a teaspoon if vanilla essence

Mix the margarine and the sugar and make a paste.

Add the carrot, flour and essence.

Put biscuit shaped bits of the mix on a greased baking sheet. Add a little sugar on top. Cook in a preheated oven at 190C/375F for 25 minutes.

Cream

Ingredients

2 and a half tablespoons of cornflour/cornstarch
350ml/11 fl oz
56g/2 oz of margarine
vanilla essence

Put the cornflour and milk in a pan and mix. Cook on a medium heat stirring all the time for 10 minutes.

Mix the margarine and sugar together. Add to the liquid with some vanilla essence. Whisk to make a cream like mix.

Icing

Ingredients

4 and half tablespoons of sugar
6 and a half tablespoons of dried milk
vanilla essence
2 tablespoon of water

Put the water in a pan with the sugar. Heat until the sugar has dissolved.

Take off the heat.

Add the milk stirring constantly. Add some vanilla essence.

Economy Cake

Ingredients

85g/3 oz of margarine
85g/3 oz of sugar
2 and a half tablespoons of golden syrup
85g/3 oz of cocoa powder
200g/7 oz of dried breadcrumbs
vanilla essence

Put the breadcrumbs in a preheated moderate oven and cook for 8 minutes.

Put the sugar, syrup and margarine in a pan. Cook on a low heat for 8 minutes to melt the margarine. Remove from heat. Add the breadcrumbs, vanilla and cocoa powder and mix.

Grease a cake tin with margarine. Add the mix. Leave for 5 hours before putting on a plate.

Christmas Cake

Ingredients

250g/8.8 oz of raisins
3 tablespoons of butter
400g/14 oz of flour
half a teaspoon of cinnamon
4 tablespoons of cocoa
1 teaspoon of sodium bicarbonate/baking soda
1 teaspoon of allspice
half a teaspoon of salt
400g/14 oz of sugar
480ml/2 cups of water

Put the butter, sugar, raisins and water in a pan. Boil for 6 minutes. Put the mix in a bowl.

Add the rest of the ingredients and mix well.

Grease a cake tin. Add the mix. Cook in a preheated oven at 176C/350F for 2 hours - for the last 35 minutes put some tin foil over the top of the cake.

Marzipan

Ingredients

1 teaspoon of almond essence
56g/2 oz of golden syrup
56g/2 oz of flour
2 tablespoons of margarine
1 tablespoon of water

Put the margarine in the water and mix. Add the syrup and almond essence and mix. Stir in the flour to make a dough. Knead for 5 minutes. Cut the marzipan as needed.

Beetroot Dessert

Ingredients

141g/5 oz of grated beetroot
198g/7 oz of flour
56g/2 oz of sugar
2 tablespoons of margarine
4 tablespoons of milk
1 teaspoon of sodium bicarbonate/baking powder

Mix the ingredients to make a dough.

Put the mix in a greased baking dish. Cook in a preheated oven at 176C/350F for 40 minutes.

Serve hot or cold.

Carrolade

Ingredients

grated rutabaga/swede
grated carrot

Squeeze the liquid from the swede and carrot into a bowl. Add some water to the juice.

Fruit Tea

Ingredients

jam
hot water

Put a teaspoon of jam in a cup of hot water.

Apple Water

Ingredients

1 litre/4 cups of water
peel from 2 apples
1 teaspoon of sugar
1 tablespoon of grated carrot

Put the ingredients in a pan and bring to the boil. Cook on a low heat for 20 minutes. Serve cool.

www.ingramcontent.com/pod-product-compliance
Ingram Content Group UK Ltd.
Pitfield, Milton Keynes, MK11 3LW, UK
UKHW010720081225
9431UKWH00041B/480